HOW TO SURVIVE A
TORNADO

KENNY ABDO

Bolt!
An Imprint of Abdo Zoom
abdopublishing.com

abdopublishing.com

Published by Abdo Zoom, a division of ABDO, P.O. Box 398166, Minneapolis, Minnesota 55439. Copyright © 2019 by Abdo Consulting Group, Inc. International copyrights reserved in all countries. No part of this book may be reproduced in any form without written permission from the publisher. Bolt!™ is a trademark and logo of Abdo Zoom.

Printed in the United States of America, North Mankato, Minnesota.
052018
092018

THIS BOOK CONTAINS
RECYCLED MATERIALS

Photo Credits: Alamy, AP Images, Getty Images, iStock, Shutterstock
Production Contributors: Kenny Abdo, Jennie Forsberg, Grace Hansen
Design Contributors: Dorothy Toth, Neil Klinepier

Library of Congress Control Number: 2017960653

Publisher's Cataloging-in-Publication Data

Names: Abdo, Kenny, author.
Title: How to survive a tornado / by Kenny Abdo.
Description: Minneapolis, Minnesota : Abdo Zoom, 2019. | Series: How to survive |
    Includes online resources and index.
Identifiers: ISBN 9781532123276 (lib.bdg.) | ISBN 9781532124259 (ebook) |
    ISBN 9781532124747 (Read-to-me ebook)
Subjects: LCSH: Survival--Juvenile literature. | Tornadoes--Juvenile literature. |
    Emergencies--Planning--Juvenile literature. | Natural disasters--
    Juvenile literature.
Classification: DDC 613.69--dc23

TABLE OF CONTENTS

TORNADOES

A tornado is a violently spinning **funnel** that grows from a thunderstorm cloud down to earth. Lightning and hail are common during a tornado. Tornadoes can strike in any season, but mostly happen in the spring and summer months.

5

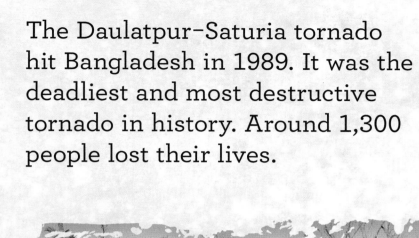

The Daulatpur-Saturia tornado hit Bangladesh in 1989. It was the deadliest and most destructive tornado in history. Around 1,300 people lost their lives.

PREPARE

Being aware of warning signs will help you be prepared. A yellow-green sky, strong winds, and low, dark clouds can mean a tornado is looming. It is important to know the difference between a **tornado watch** and a **tornado warning**.

Talk about tornadoes with your family. Discussing ahead of time helps reduce fear and panic. Make sure everyone knows where to go if there is a **tornado warning**.

Having a survival kit is key. It should include water, canned food, and a whistle. A flashlight and extra batteries will help if power is lost.

DISASTER PREP

- WATER
- NON-PERISHABLE FOOD
- BATTERY RADIO
- BATTERIES
- FIRST AID KIT
- FLASHLIGHT

ARATION LIST

- **TRASH BAGS**
- **MATCHES**
- **WHISTLE**
- **CASH & KEYS**
- **HAND SANITIZER**
- **BASIC TOOL SET**

13

SURVIVE

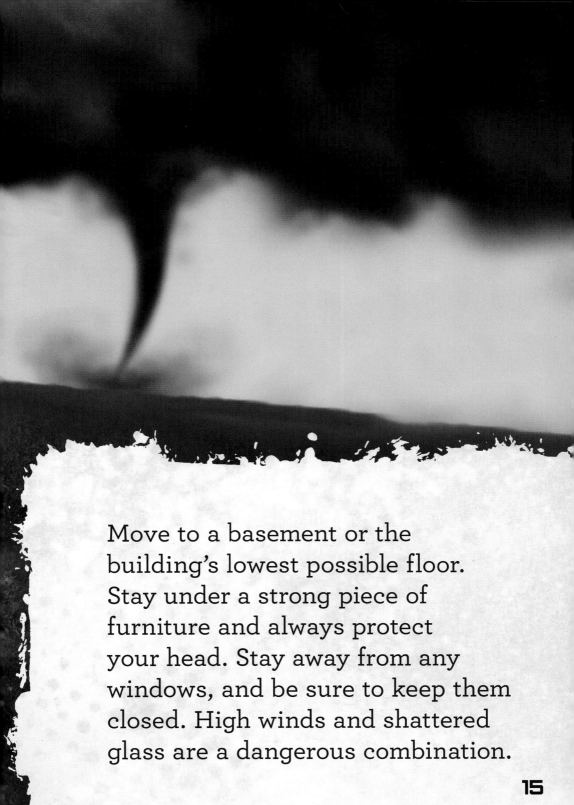

Move to a basement or the building's lowest possible floor. Stay under a strong piece of furniture and always protect your head. Stay away from any windows, and be sure to keep them closed. High winds and shattered glass are a dangerous combination.

If you are stuck outside, find a **ditch** in the ground, lie flat, and cover your head. Watch for flying **debris**, as it causes the most harm during tornadoes.

If you are driving, leave your vehicle and enter a building. If there are no buildings around, find a **ditch** in the ground and lie flat. Do not seek shelter under a highway **overpass**.

When the tornado passes, let friends and family know you are safe. Continue listening to local news or radio for updated information and instructions. If you are trapped, use a whistle to signal your location.